MJHCC 20012

DATE DUE

The Library of Author Biographies

S. E. Hinton

The Library of Author Biographies

S. E. HINTON

Antoine Wilson

the rosen publishing group's
rosen
central

Y
B
H I N

For Chrissy

Published in 2003 by The Rosen Publishing Group, Inc.
29 East 21st Street, New York, NY 10010

Library of Congress Cataloging-in-Publication Data

Wilson, Antoine.
S.E. Hinton / Antoine Wilson.— 1st ed.
    p. cm. — (The library of author biographies)
Summary: Discusses the life, novels, and writing habits of S.E. Hinton, author of such popular books as "The Outsiders" and "That Was Then, This Is Now."
Includes bibliographical references and index.
ISBN 0-8239-3778-X (lib. bdg.)
1. Hinton, S. E.—Juvenile literature. 2. Young adult fiction—Authorship—Juvenile literature. 3. Authors, American—20th century—Biography—Juvenile literature. [1. Hinton, S. E. 2. Authors, American. 3. Women—Biography.] I. Title. II. Series.
PS3558.I548 Z96 2002
813'.54—dc21

                                                    2002007905

Manufactured in the United States of America

Table of Contents

Introduction: What "S. E." Stands For

The first thing you should know about S. E. Hinton is that the "S. E." stands for Susan Eloise, and that Susan Eloise Hinton is a woman. Most readers guess that S. E. Hinton is a man when they read her books. And why not? The main characters of all of her novels are male, and the stories are told by boys. The action, which can get pretty violent, often revolves around boys fighting with other boys. The female characters don't seem to get as much attention as the boys, especially in Hinton's first few novels.

But, probably the main reason people think Hinton is a man is that she goes by "S. E."

instead of "Susan Eloise" or "Susie." Don't worry if you were fooled; actually, you're kind of supposed to think Hinton is a man. The decision to use her initials was made by her publishers, who didn't necessarily want to advertise the fact that the writer of these tough-boy stories was a young woman. More on that decision in chapter 1.

The second thing you should know is that Susan Eloise Hinton is a private person. Some writers, like Norman Mailer (author of *The Executioner's Song*, 1979), live very public lives and are known for the things they do as well as the books they write. They enjoy the celebrity of being a famous writer. Other writers, like J. D. Salinger (author of *Catcher in the Rye*, 1951) want to keep their private lives as far away from public scrutiny as they can. They want their books to speak for themselves. Hinton probably belongs to the second camp more than the first. She is not interested in the spotlight. She would rather keep her personal and family life out of the public eye.

Hinton was born in Tulsa, Oklahoma, on July 22, 1950, although some sources cite her birth year as 1948 or 1949. (The confusion about her birth year might have come about early in her career. As Hinton says, "I began the first draft of *The Outsiders* when I was fifteen. Nobody believes that, so I usually say sixteen. My editors say seventeen, just in case."[1]) She grew up in Tulsa, and aside from three years in northern California and six months in Spain, she has spent her whole life there. Her passions—horseback riding, reading, and writing—have remained much as they were when she was a kid.

Even though her interests have remained the same, and even though she has stayed in the same place most of her life, Hinton's life has been remarkable. In her late teen years, she went from being an unassuming tomboy to being one of the most successful young adult authors ever. In the process, she started a completely new trend in young adult literature, writing realistic and gritty books for teenagers that speak to what it really feels like to be a teen. Add to that the fact that her first novel was accepted for publication on the day of her high school graduation. How many people can you say that about? Most writers get their first novels published well after they have graduated from college, if they are lucky enough to get their books published at all.

Hinton's first book, *The Outsiders* (1967), became a huge worldwide success and publishing phenomenon. She followed it with three more novels, one coming out every four years: *That Was Then, This Is Now* (1971), *Rumble Fish* (1975), and *Tex* (1979). Another novel, *Taming the Star Runner* (1988), came out nine years after *Tex*. She has also written two children's books, *The Puppy Sister* (1995) and *Big David, Little David* (1995).

Even now, over thirty years after it was first published, people are still reading *The Outsiders*. It is a classic that gets passed down from generation to generation. Not many books have this kind of staying power. What is it that keeps Hinton's books from seeming out of date? One possible reason is that she avoids writing about things that are topical. In other words, rather than focusing on something that is currently a "hot" issue, she writes about those things that don't change much over time, like what it feels like to be a teenager.

It doesn't really matter whether she's writing about gangs or horses—Hinton knows the inner workings of teenage lives very well. Her main characters—Ponyboy, Bryon, Rusty-James, Tex, and Travis, to name a few—remain alive to us because they seem real. As she said in a 1983 interview, "I don't know what the latest hot trend is. I hate the 'problem' approach. Problems change. Character remains the same. I write character."[2] Character endures, and even if certain details seem outdated, Hinton's books still hit us where it counts.

1 "I Wanted Something to Read"

Susan Eloise Hinton began writing *The Outsiders* during her sophomore year at Will Rogers High School in Tulsa, Oklahoma. Even though *The Outsiders* was her first published work, it was actually her third novel. She had written two novels—neither of which were published—all before the tenth grade. She had been writing since the third grade, and her stories before *The Outsiders* had been almost completely focused on cowboys and horses. This includes her first two unpublished novels, which she claims to have written because she "had read all the cowboy and horse books in the library" and she "wanted something to read."[1] (As this quote reveals, S. E. Hinton is very modest when she talks about her writing. She usually prefers to make a joke of something rather than get into how hard she works.)

Even though those books will probably never get published, they form an important part of Hinton's writing career—the part in which she was teaching herself to write. Many writers have to write a few books before they write one that they can sell. It usually takes them a few tries to figure out how to do it. And, even then, writing a novel is not an easy thing to do. In fact, some people spend their whole lives trying to write a good novel. Meanwhile, it took Hinton only a year and a half to write *The Outsiders*, and she went through four complete drafts of the novel in that time.

Hinton's process for *The Outsiders* was to write a first draft of forty pages, then go back to that draft to rewrite and add details. As she has said, "I happily wrote *The Outsiders* over and over again, not knowing what I was doing."[2] Hinton was enjoying the freedom of being a beginner. Nobody expected her to write anything great, and she was mainly trying to keep herself entertained.

Or so she would have you think. In fact, she might have had some literary ambitions in the back of her mind. Hinton had a friend whose mother was a writer, and Hinton showed her the manuscript when she felt it was done. Her friend's mother then gave Hinton the name of an agent in New York. The agent read it and liked it, and sold the book to the second publisher he tried, Viking Press in New York City.

Getting a novel published is not usually that easy, especially for an unknown teenage writer. Then again, no one had seen anything quite like *The Outsiders* before. Hinton wrote it because she felt that all of the books written for kids her age were not realistic—they just didn't ring true. She had moved beyond the cowboy and horse books in search of good teenage books, and she was very disappointed in what she found.

In an interview with *Seventeen* magazine, Hinton said, "I'd wanted to read books that showed teenagers outside the life of 'Mary Jane went to the prom.'"[3] The books available to her did not deal with the real lives of teenagers, but with a fantasy world in which everything was perfect and where characters did not have real-life problems. Hinton's response to the situation, as she relayed it, gives us a clue to her personality, and echoes her earlier response to the lack of cowboy and horse books: "When I couldn't find any [good teenage books], I decided to write one myself. I created a world with no adult authority figures, where kids lived by their own rules."[4]

This is the world of *The Outsiders*, and the world of most of Hinton's novels. Teenage kids living on their own, without adult supervision and without any rules. However, this world is no fun-filled fantasy. The kids have to figure out their own rules the hard way, and the lack of adult authority figures makes their lives harder, not easier. In a way, this is where Hinton's so-called gritty realism comes from. While most readers of her books will never see a knife fight, much less participate in one, the books seem very realistic. And while most readers of her books do have authority figures and rules to contend with, her books depict a heightened version of the typical teenage experience: rebelling against authority while trying to figure things out for yourself.

While writing *The Outsiders*, Hinton had difficulties of her own. Her father was diagnosed with a brain tumor in her sophomore year of high school, as she was beginning the book. He died in her junior year, around the time she was finishing the book. It's possible that young Susie turned to writing *The Outsiders* as a way of coping with her father's illness. In a 1967 article in the *Tulsa Daily World*, Hinton's mother said that "Susie was very close to her father, and I noticed the sicker he became, the harder she worked."[5] The loss of her father could also be partly why the emotions in *The Outsiders* and her other novels seem so urgent. The fantasy of a world without adults can be a nightmare for those who are actually going through the death of a parent, and Hinton might have sensed that losing her father meant that she would have to figure out more things by herself. The theme of teenagers figuring things out on their own is dominant in all of Hinton's young adult novels, and is perhaps most central to *The Outsiders*.

2 *The Outsiders* (1967)

The novel *The Outsiders* deals with a subject known to just about anyone who has ever gone to a large high school: the battle between two rival groups of kids. In the novel, the rival groups are the poor, scrappy greasers and the rich, fancy socs (short for "socials"). These types of rival groups exist in many high schools, even though different high schools have different names for the groups. Regardless of the names, the struggles are often similar.

Although Hinton did not belong to either group at her school, she got to see firsthand the way the groups dealt with each other. Mainly, she felt angry about the way the socs treated the greasers, driving by and yelling things at them, or worse. She reacted to the situation in her own way, by writing about it. In an article, Hinton said, "It was the cold-blooded beating of a friend of mine that gave me the idea of writing a book."[1]

While the inspiration to write *The Outsiders* came from the world around her, Hinton did not simply write the story of what was going on in her school. She did what many great writers do—she took the raw material of life, combined it with imagination and hard work, and made a fictional story out of it.

Hinton approached the conflict between the greasers and the socs through the interaction of her central characters. Some writers like to come up with a story or plot first, and then fill in character details along the way. Hinton's process is the reverse—she starts with characters and discovers the plot later. She likes to get to know her characters really well, including what they look like, what they like to eat, and when their birthdays are. In fact, sometimes she will fill many pages exploring the details of a relatively minor character, even though she knows the pages will probably not appear in the final manuscript. As a result, she often knows facts about her characters that might not end up appearing in the book. This helps her understand her characters' motivations, or why they do what they do.

In a press release from her publisher, Hinton said, "There is an interesting transformation that takes place in the beginning of a book. I go straight from thinking about my narrator to being him."[2] Like an actor, Hinton likes to inhabit her characters, except that she's also making up all of the lines as she goes. This type of approach makes sense for an author who has written four of her five novels in the first person, using an "I" narrator who tells the story.

Ponyboy Curtis was the first of her now-famous narrators, and with him, Hinton began a tradition that has raised many questions: She tends to write about a world made up of boys, and tends to let male narrators tell the story. Because of this, people are always asking, "Where are the girls?" and Hinton has tried to explain this choice several times over the years. Basically, she was a tomboy and grew up mainly around boys. Also, when she was growing up, the women's movement had not really gotten going and women did not have as many opportunities as they do today. Young women and girls in particular were expected to act according to a set of expectations. The world of girls was too limited for what Hinton wanted to do, and because of this, she wrote about boys.

She felt that if she wrote the books from the point of view of a girl, people would not believe the stories she told, so she used a male narrator instead. This decision turned out to be a good one in terms of book sales. At the time, publishers felt that girls would read books about boys, but few boys would choose to read books about girls. Somewhere along the way, her publisher decided that Susan Eloise Hinton should go by S. E. Hinton so people would not know whether she was male or female. Most readers, of course, assumed that she was a man, and she received plenty of fan letters addressed to "Mr. Hinton."

Many of the themes established in *The Outsiders* reappear in Hinton's other books in slightly different variations, and while Hinton's approach to these themes becomes more sophisticated, her concerns do not shift wildly from book to book. Two themes she returns to again and again are that growing up usually involves some painful decisions, and that the period between childhood and adulthood involves setting your own rules and learning to cope with things you cannot change. In *The Outsiders*, Ponyboy recites the poem "Nothing Gold Can Stay," by Robert Frost:

Nature's first green is gold,

her hardest hue to hold.

Her early leaf's a flower;

But only so an hour.

Then leaf subsides to leaf.

So Eden sank to grief.

So dawn comes down to day.

Nothing gold can stay.[3]

Hinton uses this poem to illustrate one of the book's main themes: the loss of innocence. To a certain extent, loss of innocence is an unavoidable part of growing up. In an interview, Hinton explained her own interpretation of "staying gold": She said, "Gold is openness to other people, an ability to empathize [to understand and share another person's thoughts, feelings, or emotions] with other human beings. I believe you're more likely to have that when you're young. You compromise as you get older."[4] One of the big questions of *The Outsiders* is whether Ponyboy will be able to maintain his "openness" in the face of the harsh realities around him.

Now that *The Outsiders* is such a classic, it is easy to assume that the book started flying off the shelves as soon as it was published. However, that wasn't the case. The sales were slow at first, but then word started to spread and sales grew and grew. Apparently, Hinton had not only written the book she wanted to read, but a book that thousands of kids wanted to read, too. (Thousands, and eventually millions. Today, *The Outsiders* has over eight million copies in print.)

Hinton had tapped into a whole new generation of readers, young people who had been waiting for a writer to come along and tell stories about their world, in a voice that seemed like their own. She had quietly revolutionized young adult publishing by writing about what it really felt like to be a teenager, and by depicting Ponyboy's inner emotions, the harsh world around him, and the gap between the two.

The reviews for the book were mostly positive. Some reviewers criticized the novel for being overly sentimental or for having a plot that seemed overly convenient. Some readers felt that certain events in the book, rather than building upon previous events, seemed forced or out of place. For instance, the church fire that helps to propel the book toward its conclusion was jarring to some. The presence of trapped children in the burning church—which, a chapter before had been Ponyboy and Johnny's hideout—did not seem realistic. To some critics, it felt as if the schoolchildren had been placed there simply so that Ponyboy and Johnny could do something heroic. Others commented that the book was full of clichés—ideas that had been expressed so many times they did not seem sincere any more. But the book was sincere, and most critics recognized that Hinton's approach to the class differences in the greaser versus soc rivalry, along with her ability to depict Ponyboy's voice, would have an effect on young audiences regardless of the literary qualities they used to judge other books.

Most of the reviewers were impressed by what this teenage wonder was able to write. Writer Nat Hentoff, in the magazine, *Atlantic Monthly*, praised Hinton's authenticity and energy, stating that she had "an astute ear and a lively sense of the restless rhythms of the young."[5] In the *New York Times Book Review*, Thomas Fleming set aside the fact that Hinton was a teenager and wrote, "By almost any standard, Miss Hinton's performance is impressive."[6]

The best reactions came from the fans. Some of Hinton's fan letters were reprinted in a 1968 article in a magazine called the *Saturday Review*, and these letters provide an intriguing look at how the book was received by its intended audience. From a fourteen-year-old girl: "I feel that all teen-agers from all environments should read this novel. It would give people a better understanding of these troubled teen-agers and not judge them by their long hair and odd ways." From a fourteen-year-old boy: "In presentation this story seemed very true to life as I know those kind of circumstances prevail in many N.Y. areas." A high school junior states, "At school we have socs and greasers except we do not call them by those names. We call our socs cliques. Our greasers are hards." Finally, from a letter addressed to "Mr. Hinton": "If you are really Ponyboy, and you have been through these ordeals, God must really love you."[7]

Some adults, of course, objected to the violence in the book. Others complained that the book was sensationalist, or written just to create a scandal and make some money. Some even suggested that the book was not written by a real teenager. They complained that the book could make teenagers more violent, or expose readers to violence they were not ready to deal with. Hinton's refreshing response still applies today. In an article, she wrote, "Adults who let small children watch hours of violence . . . on TV, scream their heads off when a book written for children contains a fist fight."[8]

Hinton's book was threatening to many adults, if only because it wasn't the sort of "Mary Jane goes to the prom" book they were used to. But Hinton wasn't interested in writing about following the rules and finding happiness; she wrote about dealing with the stress of being a teenager in a world without obvious rules or reliable adult guidance.

Despite what some adults had to say, the book was a commercial and critical success. *The Outsiders* was selected as one of the *New York Herald Tribune*'s Best Teenage Books for 1967, and was a *Chicago Tribune Book World* Spring Book Festival Honor Book that same year. In 1975, it was awarded a Media and Methods Maxi Award, and was named one of the Best Young Adult Books by the American Library Association. Finally, in 1979, it was recognized with a Massachusetts Children's Book Award. In 1983, it was made into a movie starring C. Thomas Howell and Matt Dillon. (See chapters 7 and 8 for more on the movie versions of Hinton's books.)

By the time she was seventeen, S. E. Hinton was a success. She was in her freshman year of college at the University of Tulsa. She was able to pay for part of her education with royalties (payment for sales) from her book. But being a teenage author was not all glamour and glory. In a 1981 interview with *Seventeen* magazine, Hinton said that people who did not know her started treating her as though she was "stuck-up."

She explained further: "I had always been a smart-alecky kid, but after the book was published, I knew I had to change, or else people would think success was going to my head. So I became quiet—but people saw that as being stuck-up, too."[9]

Whether she liked it or not, her book was a publishing phenomenon, and she was famous. With publication, payment, and fame came the pressure of being a professional author, from whom something great would now be expected.

3 *That Was Then, This Is Now* (1971)

Suddenly the teenage tomboy Susie Hinton had become the famous novelist S. E. Hinton. With the success of *The Outsiders* came some things she wasn't expecting: interviews, book tours, lots of young fans with lots of questions for her. She was now a professional writer, no longer working by herself on stories no one else would read. Everyone wanted to know what she was going to write next, including Hinton herself. She was ready to get started on another novel, but there was only one problem: She couldn't write.

Writer's block, which happens to most writers at some time in their careers, occurs when, for one reason or another, people who have written a book (or maybe even a dozen), find themselves unable to write. Sometimes it's because a writer may feel that he or she has run out of ideas. Other times, he or she may have just become tired of writing day-in, day-out. More often than not, though, writer's block strikes when a writer feels that a project is impossible, or is doomed to fail no matter what he or she does. It can happen simply because writing is so difficult, and the writer keeps putting off a project until the next day. It can also happen when a writer is trying to live up to high expectations.

Here's what Hinton had to say about her writer's block in a interview: "Right off I had writer's block for years. I couldn't even write a letter. It was like everybody was waiting to see what this teenage wonder was going to do next. The next one had to be a masterpiece."[1] Hinton had written *The Outsiders* in a vacuum: She had simply let the story and its characters take her away into another world. She took it seriously, but she also made sure to enjoy herself; sometimes, when she got stuck on a plot detail, she would ask her friends at school what should happen next. The only pressure on her was the pressure she put on herself. After all, no one was expecting anything from her. All this had changed, though, since the publication of that first novel.

On top of all the big expectations, Hinton was being exposed to a range of great literature. She was at college, and suddenly she was reading books she had never read before. She read many good writers, and her first thought was "Oh, no." As she said in an interview, "I read *The Outsiders* again when I was 20, and I thought it was the worst piece of trash I'd ever seen. I magnified all its faults."[2]

At the University of Tulsa, Hinton majored in education and considered a career in teaching. Trying to become a teacher seemed logical at the time, as she had always enjoyed the company of kids. As part of her program, she did some student teaching, but she started to think that maybe it was not the right career for her. She found it exhausting, both physically and emotionally. Hinton found that when she came home from teaching, she continued to worry about the kids and their problems. To top it off, she began to feel depressed. She was a writer, after all, and she wasn't doing any writing. This was where David Inhofe came in.

Hinton and Inhofe met in a freshman biology class and started dating soon afterward. Inhofe (who would eventually become Hinton's husband) became concerned about Hinton being depressed all the time. He knew the solution: She had to write. And while the best stuff often comes from a writer who is inspired and feeling creative, nothing comes from a writer who isn't writing. Inhofe understood this, and he came up with a strategy to get his girlfriend to write again. Hinton had to write two pages a day, simple as that. He knew that as long as she was writing, she wouldn't be depressed.

As Hinton explained it in an autobiographical sketch: "David made me write *That Was Then, This is Now*. When I was writing for fun, I loved it; when it turned into a profession it scared me. I kept thinking 'You don't know what you're doing.' I wrote *That Was Then* over a period of three or four months, two pages a day, never looking back. David was my boyfriend at the time; if I didn't get my two pages done, we didn't go out."[3]

Soon, Hinton was too busy on her new book to be depressed about not writing. Even though she didn't feel confident while writing *That Was Then, This Is Now*, it was clear that writing *The Outsiders* had taught her a thing or two about writing a novel. She had learned that discipline and good writing habits are part of the equation. As she said in a talk at the Boston Public Library, "I was very careful with this book, and I wanted each sentence to be exactly right, and I'd just sweat out my two pages, and I'd put them in a stack."[4] Then, with her work done for the day, she and David would go out.

It wasn't long before Hinton had a novel-sized manuscript ready to go to the publisher. She sent it off and it was accepted immediately. Not only that, the editors did not require her to do any major rewriting. The manuscript, with only minor changes, became *That Was Then, This Is Now*. This, as much as anything, is proof of the discipline with which she approached writing those two pages every day.

Inhofe had helped her get out of her depression and back into writing, and Hinton had stuck with it until her book was done. She was exhausted from the publication of *The*

Outsiders and from the writing of *That Was Then, This Is Now*. She needed a break. She and David got married in September 1970 and went off to Europe for a while, to relax on the southern coast of Spain.

That Was Then, This Is Now is narrated by Bryon Douglas, who in many ways is similar to Ponyboy. He's not a bad kid, really, just caught up in some bad circumstances. One source of his trouble is Mark Jennings, his best friend. Mark lives with Bryon and Bryon's mother because he's an orphan; his parents killed each other in a fight. Bryon's mother is in the hospital, so the boys basically have the house to themselves. Once again, Hinton creates a world in which kids are left alone to learn difficult life lessons without the help of their parents.

The setting is the same as in *The Outsiders*, and Ponyboy Curtis even makes an appearance, sparking a fight that lands Mark in a hospital emergency room. Maybe Hinton liked Ponyboy too much to let him go. Maybe she just wanted to connect this novel to *The Outsiders* to let careful readers know she was writing about the same world she'd created in the first book. Either way, Ponyboy was back, and fans of *The Outsiders* could get excited about the possibility of seeing him from another point of view. The view is especially interesting because Bryon doesn't like Ponyboy.

While *The Outsiders* was concerned with the loss of innocence and "staying gold," *That Was Then, This Is Now* takes a slightly different approach to the way people change over time. Instead of focusing on one character's attempt to keep his innocence in a topsy-turvy world, Hinton takes a more sophisticated approach in this second book: She looks at how Bryon and Mark's friendship changes over time. In other words, rather than being about one character's relationship to the world, this book is about the relationship between two characters. The title says it all. Sometimes people go in different directions and never meet again. Different approaches to this theme appeared in Hinton's next two novels.

Whether the reviewers liked the book or not, they noticed the discipline Hinton had put into writing her new novel—the structure of the book was more controlled and the characters' actions seemed more thought-out than in *The Outsiders*. Some critics said that her style was beginning to mature, that she was on her way to becoming a serious novelist. Others missed the young, raw energy of *The Outsiders*. They thought *That Was Then, This Is Now* was too controlled, too emotionally cool.

Michael Cart, writing in the *New York Times Book Review*, praised Hinton's handling of theme in the book: "The phrase 'if only' is perhaps the most bittersweet in the language, and Miss Hinton uses it skillfully to underline her theme: growth can be a dangerous process." He wrote that *That Was Then, This Is Now* was "a mature, disciplined novel, which excites a response in the reader. Whatever its faults, the book will be hard to forget."[5] Sheryl Andrews wrote in *Horn Book* magazine that the book "will speak directly to a large number of teen-agers and does have a place in the understanding of today's cultural problems."[6]

Hinton continued her string of awards with the publication of *That Was Then, This Is Now*. The book received an ALA Best Books for Young Adults citation in 1971, and was a *Chicago Tribune Book World* Spring Book Festival Award Honor Book that same year; it also received a Massachusetts Children's Book Award in 1978.

That Was Then, This Is Now was the book Hinton had to write in order to keep going. Now no one could say she was just a one-hit wonder. No one could dismiss *The Outsiders* as a fluke or as a publicity scheme. S. E. Hinton was a serious writer.

4 Rumble Fish (1975)

In between writing *The Outsiders* and *That Was Then, This Is Now*, Hinton wrote a short story called "Rumble Fish." She published it in a magazine called *Nimrod*, which was a supplement to the *University of Tulsa Alumni Magazine*. The short story she wrote has most of the elements that the book *Rumble Fish* contains.

Hinton got the idea for the story from a picture she'd cut out of a magazine sometime around 1967. The picture was of a boy and a motorcycle. Something about the image fascinated Hinton. (Apparently she still has the picture, which she keeps in a frame.) By the time *Rumble Fish* was published, she couldn't even remember what magazine the picture had come from.

Having a finished short story in hand would seem to make writing the novel easier than starting from scratch. After all, she only had to expand the short story, right? If only things were that easy. For Hinton, the major problem with writing this book was trying to decide on her narrator, the character who would tell the story. The short story moved around from character to character, but for the novel, Hinton wanted one character to tell the story, like in her first two novels. Apparently, she wrote an entire draft of the novel, from page one to the end, with straight-laced Steve as the narrator. It wasn't good enough for her. As Hinton explained, "I already had the book done, and I read it over and just couldn't stand it. It was too easy, he was too intelligent, he was too articulate, too observant."[1]

Hinton was looking for a challenge. She got the idea to have the troubled Rusty-James tell the story, instead of the well-spoken Steve. In Rusty-James, she was trying to create a character who could not explain everything about himself. This was a challenge because, unlike the narrators of her previous books, Ponyboy and Bryon, this narrator wasn't going to be as good at expressing himself or as aware of his emotions. Hinton wanted the novel to be about the way Rusty-James identifies with his older brother Motorcycle Boy (a legendary street gang fighter) without being able to understand him.

The life of a writer can seem glamorous to some, but Hinton's life is simple. As she describes it, "A writer's life is not very exciting—usually you're alone in a room with your tools—paper, pen, imagination."[2] She was equally honest about facing up to the challenge of writing this third book: "*Rumble Fish* was written on Thursday nights, because that was when my husband played poker."[3] David Inhofe had remained a positive force when it came to Hinton's writing. In an interview, Hinton said, "I like to have him read what I'm working on, but only to tell me that he likes it. I don't want anybody criticizing my work while I'm doing it. But every once in a while he makes some good suggestions."[4] The artistic process is fragile, and having someone nearby who can

Attention to Detail

Here's a fun exercise: After you've read *Rumble Fish*, go back to the first chapter and read it again. (Good novels are usually worth reading more than once.) You'll notice how skillfully Hinton drops in all kinds of hints about who Rusty-James and Steve have become, one of them not doing much with his life, the other attending college.

give positive reinforcement can be very helpful. Criticism at the wrong time can send writers into a panic.

One thing readers of *Rumble Fish* notice is its interesting structure. The first chapter and the last chapter happen after the main story has already occurred. Rusty-James runs into his old friend Steve down by the beach. A lot has happened to him since they last saw each other, and seeing Steve reminds him of the story that makes up the bulk of the novel. It's as if Hinton has taken the whole *That Was Then, This Is Now* theme (friends whose lives are going in different directions) and used it to tell another story. Framing the book with these two chapters is a bold move. Hinton uses a so-called flashback narrative, one in which part of the story's end comes first, followed by the events that led up to it. There's always the risk that some readers will get confused by the shift in time, but in *Rumble Fish*, that risk pays off. It gives Hinton the freedom, as a writer, to tell us the end before we read the whole story. That scene on the beach stays with us the whole time we are reading, even if we don't think of it. (We know, for instance, that whatever happens to Rusty-James, he's not going to die.) This way, Hinton gets to focus on how things happen rather than what is going to happen.

The reviews of *Rumble Fish* were mixed, not because people's reactions were lukewarm, but because some reviewers loved the book and others really did not like it at all. The opinions ranged from a *Publishers Weekly* review claiming that Hinton was a "brilliant novelist,"[5] to a *Kirkus* review that said that Hinton "seems to have no more of a future, or even a present, than Rusty-James has."[6]

Jane Powell, in the *Times Literary Supplement*, found the book "a disappointment." Her reasons are interesting and relate to Rusty-James's not being able to fully understand his situation. Powell wrote, "The earlier two books [*The Outsiders* and *That Was Then, This Is Now*] also deal with the American delinquent scene, but in both the central character has an intelligence and sensitivity which set him apart from his peers . . . [Rusty-James] involves himself in situations largely out of loyalty to others and at the end . . . is left wiser and sadder."[7] (By "delinquent scene," Powell means Hinton's world of rebellious, rule-breaking teenagers.) Powell's complaint about the character of Rusty-James implies that she would like him to be a bit more like Ponyboy or Bryon.

On the other hand, Margery Fisher, in a review in the magazine *Growing Point*, called *Rumble Fish* "a book as uncompromising in its view of life as it is disciplined in form . . . Of the three striking books by this young author, *Rumble Fish* seems the most carefully structured and the most probing."[8] ("Uncompromising" refers to the way that Hinton is willing to make her characters' problems as difficult as real-life problems, without sugar-coating things.) Fisher seemed to like exactly what Powell complained about.

Why the difference of opinion? Jay Daly, in his book about Hinton's work, *Presenting S. E. Hinton* (1989), had this to say about *Rumble Fish*: "The success or failure of this book rests with its ability to bring the reader into contact, not so much with the motivations of the characters or the answers to their particular problems, but with the mythic sense of life itself, with the element of mystery for which there are no answers but belief."[9] Readers who tapped into that "element of mystery" were excited to see Hinton moving in new, more ambitious directions. Readers who were looking for more of the same were disappointed by Hinton's desire to tackle larger questions.

Whatever the critics had to say, *Rumble Fish* received many awards, among them an American Library Association Best Books for Young Adults citation in 1975. It was also named one of the Best Books of the Year by the *School Library Journal* in 1975, and received a Land of Enchantment Book Award from the New Mexico Library Association in 1982 ("Land of Enchantment" is New Mexico's state motto).

Hinton considers *Rumble Fish* to be her most literary book. She calls it the easiest to read, but the hardest to understand. Of all of her books, this is the one she recommends her readers come back to when they're older.

5 *Tex* (1979)

T he novel *Tex* is the crowning achievement of Hinton's first four books. The book was also one of the most difficult to write, because Hinton had set a new challenge for herself: to write a book focused on relationships in which the events seem natural and realistic, and in which the central character (Tex McCormick) becomes more mature by the end of the book.

After experimenting with the non-self-aware Rusty-James in *Rumble Fish*, Hinton returned to a more typical Hinton narrator, though one who was more mature than Ponyboy or Bryon. In a press release from her publisher, Hinton had this to say about Tex McCormick: He is "perhaps the most childlike character I've ever done, but the one who makes the greatest strides toward maturity. I have to admit he's a favorite child."[1] Unlike Ponyboy, who tended to think similar to how young Hinton thought, Tex McCormick is a fully fleshed-out character who is significantly different from Hinton. Creating such a character is a challenge for any writer, and Hinton combined this challenge with the desire to make a novel that seemed realistic and smooth, and which didn't rely on big, flashy plot events (such as the church fire near the end of *The Outsiders*) to keep readers interested.

Hinton has said that Tex McCormick was the narrator she most enjoyed "being." She described Tex this way: "Capable of thinking, he has to be made to think; he relies on instinct instead of intellect. And basically his instincts are good. Capable of violence, but not malice, he has to learn things the hard way—a basically happy person trying to deal with unhappiness. I envied his total lack of suspicion."[2]

It's not surprising that of all her novels, *Tex* took Hinton the longest to write. She spent three and a half years just plotting it, or figuring out the events that would make up the core of the book. She was not suffering from writer's block, as she had with *That Was Then, This Is Now*; rather, Hinton took so long to write *Tex* because she wanted it to be good. She took the time to construct the novel very carefully so that it would seem smooth, natural, and unforced.

Hinton had the luxury of time and the maturity to know how to take advantage of that luxury. In an interview, Hinton talked about her writing process: "The beginning is kind of easy because you can put characters in any situation. Getting from point A to Z is just so hard for me, and I get off on tangents and write 50 pages on a minor character. So I think, this isn't going to be the direction I thought, and I tear it up. What's going to happen next? I need to get 'Tex' from there over here, but how do I do that? Sometimes I put it away for months at a time."[3] You can see here why Hinton downplays the "glamour" of a writer's life in interviews—writing a novel can be a difficult and frustrating process, with lots of false starts and dead ends.

During this process, Hinton's husband, David, offered his help when he could. As usual, he provided positive feedback during the process of drafting the novel. In fact, as Hinton told the *Los Angeles Times* in an interview, "One of the best lines in *Tex* was given to me by David. It's where some woman television reporter is sort of taken with how good looking Tex is and asks him where he got those cute dimples. Tex tells her—and this is David's line—'Oh, God gave me my face, but He let me pick my nose.'"[4]

The world of *Tex* is one familiar to any Hinton reader: teenage boys trying to get by without parents around. Fourteen-year-old Tex McCormick lives with his brother, Mason. Their mother is dead and their father is on the rodeo circuit so much that he isn't around to take care of the boys. Since they have financial problems, Mason has to sell off their horses—including Tex's horse, Negrito—to pay the bills. Tex is enraged by Mason's decision to sell the horses, in part because he doesn't yet understand adult responsibilities such as having to pay bills.

Much of the story focuses on Tex and Mason's relationship. The two brothers are headed in different directions, and one of the book's central themes can be summed up in a fortune teller's prediction for Tex's future: "There are people who go, people who stay. You will stay."[5] Unlike *That Was Then, This Is Now* and *Rumble Fish*, though, *Tex* ends on a more hopeful note. Mason will go and Tex will stay, but that doesn't mean that they are forever lost to each other.

Careful readers of *That Was Then, This Is Now* usually recognize Ponyboy Curtis when he reappears in that novel, but it takes a really sharp eye to spot a similar reappearance in *Tex*. The hitchhiker who kidnaps Mason and Tex is actually Mark, from *That Was Then, This Is Now*, and he has just busted out of jail.

Reviewers immediately recognized that *Tex* was an achievement for Hinton, and that her craft had continued to improve over the years. Marilyn Kaye, in a *School Library Journal* review, stated that "Hinton's style has matured since she exploded onto the young adult (YA) scene in 1967."[6] Then Kaye went on to say that Hinton's "raw energy" has not been "tamed" but "cultivated." In other words, Hinton managed to maintain her original vision while also developing it into mature art. And Margery Fisher, in *Growing Point*, wrote, "Susan Hinton has achieved that illusion of reality which any fiction writer aspires to and which few ever completely achieve."[7] In other words, she had written a book that seemed real and true without drawing any attention to its devices or its author. There is nothing out of place to distract the reader from Tex's story. This, as Hinton can tell you, is much easier said than done.

Tex received its fair share of awards, highlighting its standing among the best of Hinton's books. It received an American Library Association Best Books for Young Adults citation and a *School Library Journal* Best Books of the Year citation in 1979; a New York Public Library Books for the Teen-Age citation in 1980; an American Book Award nomination for children's paperback in 1981; and a Sue Hefly Award Honor Book Award from the Louisiana Association of School Libraries and a California Young Reader Medal nomination from the California Reading Association, both in 1982.

6 *Taming the Star Runner* (1988)

There was a long gap between the publication of *Tex* (1979) and Hinton's next book, *Taming the Star Runner* (1988). However, S. E. Hinton is not one to depend on prior successes, and this quiet stretch in her résumé represents a very busy time in her life. First of all, she was helping out with the movie adaptations of her first four novels. (See the next chapter for more on her movie-making adventures.) Something else was keeping her busy, too: a new arrival in the household. In August 1983, Hinton and her husband David Inhofe became the proud parents of Nicholas David Inhofe. Working on the movie adaptations and raising her son kept her away from novel-writing for a few years.

In 1987, the year before *Taming the Star Runner* came out, a study of Hinton's work by Jay Daly called *Presenting S. E. Hinton* was published. Having a book written about your books means that you've achieved serious recognition as a writer. Daly's book explores the themes, characters, and critical reactions to all of Hinton's books. Most important, *Presenting S. E. Hinton* takes Hinton's books seriously by examining them as literature. Even though Hinton's books sold well and were reviewed in major newspapers, no one had yet written a serious study of Hinton's work. The publication of *Presenting S. E. Hinton* was quite an honor.

Then, in 1988, Hinton received the first-ever YASD/SLJ Margaret A. Edwards Award, which is given by the Young Adult Services Division of the American Library Association and by *School Library Journal*. This award recognizes more than just one book—it recognizes a lifetime of achievement. The fact that Hinton was chosen as the first recipient shows how important her books were to the field of young adult literature.

With the publication of *The Outsiders* in 1967, Hinton had just about single-handedly transformed the entire genre. She was among the first to begin to confront the real issues teenagers were going through. Once she had proved she had staying power, Hinton's books influenced generations of readers and, perhaps of equal importance, generations of writers.

Before the Daly book, and before she received the Author Achievement Award, Hinton's reputation was already solid. For example, in a 1985 *Wilson Library Bulletin* article, Patty Campbell called S. E. Hinton a "walking YA legend," "the Queen of Young Adult Novel," and "the Grand Old Lady of YA Lit."[1] The Daly book and the YASD/SLJ Award helped to make such praise official.

The question was, of course, would Hinton be able to live up to this reputation with her new book. Would she have trouble writing about teenagers as she became older? What effect would family life have on her books? Could Hinton, now a "Grand Old Lady," still write a convincing book about teenagers?

Taming the Star Runner differs from her first four novels in a significant way: The story is no longer narrated by the main character. Hinton's previous four novels were "told" by Ponyboy, Bryon, Rusty-James, and Tex, respectively. For example, in *The Outsiders*, the whole novel is supposed to be a paper Ponyboy writes for English class. In *Taming the Star Runner*, though, the narrator stands outside the action. Travis does not tell us his story himself. Instead of being written in first-person ("I thought . . ."), the book is written in the third-person ("He thought . . ."), with Travis's thoughts and actions told by an anonymous narrator.

Some readers questioned whether Hinton was losing touch with what it felt like to be a teenager. Otherwise, why would she decide to write in the third person? Why wouldn't she dive in and "become" her main character, like she had in the other books? But it turns out that getting older didn't have much to do with her decision. Being a mother did. Nicholas was four years old when Hinton was writing the book, and four-year-olds require a lot of energy to take care of. About this period of time, Hinton said, "I was so involved with him that I didn't have the emotional space to become a completely different person."[2]

But she still wanted to write about teenagers. Shortly after the publication of *Taming the Star Runner*, Hinton had this to say: "I have kept writing about teenagers because, unlike most adults, I like them. It's an interesting time of life, chock-full of dramatic possibilities."[3]

As Hinton looked back at being a teenager—she was in her late thirties by this time—some of her interests and experiences began to seep into the novel. Travis is, after all, a writer. And a writer with a passion for horses. However, Hinton is careful to remind us that the novel is a work of fiction, and that although she couldn't have written the novel without having had certain experiences, Travis's experiences are mainly made up. She does admit, though, that some of the things that happen to Travis when he sells his first book did happen to her, such as being at home with her cat when the publisher's call came.

Hinton has always been passionate about horses. On her Web site, Hinton lists horseback riding as one of her hobbies, adding that she has done both jumping and dressage. In *Tex*, she wrote about horses a little bit. In *Taming the Star Runner*, she got to write a lot more about them.

55

Despite the long gap between this novel and the earlier ones, and the different technique used to present its story, *Taming the Star Runner* deals with many of the same themes Hinton explored in her other books. Travis Harris is a fifteen-year-old who is trying to figure out how to make his way in the world. He's had his fair share of trouble, and when he nearly kills his stepfather with a fireplace poker, he gets sent off to live with his uncle in the country. The country setting is a bit of a departure for Hinton, as is the presence of parental figures. (Travis has to deal with his Uncle Ken and his uncle's wife, Teresa.) For the most part, though, his uncle is distant and Travis is left alone.

Enter Casey Kincaid, an eighteen-year-old horse trainer who rents a barn on Travis's uncle's property. She's one of Hinton's most convincing and interesting female characters, and her relationship with Travis makes up a large part of the book. Casey is trying to tame Star Runner, the horse after whom the book is named.

Over the course of her five novels, Hinton has constantly challenged herself to go further, and *Taming the Star Runner* is no exception.

This book is clearly more complex than the others. There are realistic relationships with parents and fully formed characters (male and female), and the theme of the book cannot be summed up in a single sentence. Yet for all the maturity her writing has gained over the years, Hinton has not lost touch with one central thing: how it feels to be a teenager.

Some reviewers were frustrated by Travis. They felt that Travis lacked the go-get-'em approach of Hinton's other main characters. "On the surface, this fifteen-year-old resembles the classic misfits from the author's previous books; however, Travis lacks Tex's zest for living,"[4] wrote Charlene Strickland in the *School Library Journal*. Other reviewers praised the book, many of them noting that they were happy to see the "return" of S. E. Hinton after so many years. Patty Campbell, in the *New York Times Book Review*, noted the change in the writer's approach: "*Taming the Star Runner* is remarkable for its drive and the wry sweetness and authenticity of its voice. Gone is the golden idealism of the earlier works, perhaps because here Ms. Hinton observes, rather than participates in the innocence of her characters."[5] Campbell also notes the impact Hinton's new maturity might have on sales: "Because *Taming the Star Runner* is also a more mature and difficult work, it may not be as popular as the other Hinton books have continued to be with succeeding generations."[6]

After *Taming the Star Runner* came out, Hinton's writing focus began to change. In an article, she talked about how her life was changing her writing: "I'm older and I'm a parent. I wrote my first books in innocence . . . My writing is changing. I'm interested in putting adults and young children in my stories."[7] Her next two books, as a result, were a striking departure: children's books, featuring adults and children, and no teenagers.

7 S. E.'s Hollywood Adventure

The first Hinton book to be made into a film was *Tex* (it was released in 1982). The rights to make the movie were bought by Disney Studios, which made Hinton a little uncomfortable. She was familiar with other Disney films and what the people at Disney planned to do with her novel. She was worried that they would change her story and make a movie that wouldn't be true to the book. As she said at the time, "I'm not interested in making 'Tex Meets the Love Bug.' I've got a reputation for being realistic."[1] (*The Love Bug* was a Disney movie about a charming and mischievous Volkswagen Beetle named Herbie.) Judging from the way Hollywood has treated other screen adaptations of novels, Hinton got very lucky with *Tex*. As a matter of fact, she got lucky with the adaptations of most of her novels, as we'll see.

With *Tex*, her luck came in the form of director Tim Hunter, who wrote the screenplay with writer Charlie Haas. Hunter came to the project with an idea of what makes an S. E. Hinton novel special, and he understood that the strength of her novels should not be taken away in the film version. As he said in a *New York Times* article, "Susie deals with many of the social problems that other young adult writers confront, but in her books those problems are woven into the fabric of a realistic story. She never preaches or moralizes."[2]

The movie follows the basic plot of the book. Some parts of the movie are different, but those additions are very much in line with Tex's character. For example, in the movie, Tex intercepts Mason's college application to keep Mason from applying. Even though this does not happen in the novel, it seems like something Tex would do. Eventually, with his friend Jamie's help, Tex fills out the application. This also seems like something Tex would do.

The movie was shot in Tulsa, and Hinton was there for the shoot. Some novelists get involved with the movie adaptations of their books, and some just close their eyes and leave everything in the hands of the moviemakers. Hinton chose to work closely with Tim Hunter, finding good places to shoot and interacting with the actors.

The movie was a lucky break for actor Matt Dillon. (Dillon went on to become a major movie star, appearing in more than forty films so far, from *The Flamingo Kid* in 1984 to *There's Something About Mary* in 1998). Hinton recalled her first impression of Dillon: "Tex is a sweet little unworldly cowboy, and here was this guy who said, 'Like, man,' and told me *Rumble Fish* was his favorite book. When I get a letter from a kid who says *Rumble Fish* is his favorite book, he's usually in a reformatory."[3]

It took Hinton a little while to warm up to Dillon, but eventually they hit it off, and they got along really well. As she said, "All of a sudden, I thought, I made this kid up; I wrote this kid. He was exactly the kid I was writing about and for—really bright, doesn't fit into the system, has possibilities beyond the obvious."[4] Apparently, Hinton was not the only one who saw Dillon's potential. Dillon would eventually be cast in major roles in *The Outsiders* (released in March 1983) and *Rumble Fish* (released in October 1983) as well.

Hinton made her first foray into acting with *Tex*. She makes a brief appearance (or cameo) in the movie, playing a role she knew well from her college years when she was majoring in education: a teacher. And she's not the only Hinton "family" member to appear in the movie. Her horse, Toyota, plays the role of Tex's horse, Negrito.

The next movie version of one of her books was *The Outsiders*, which was directed by Francis Ford Coppola and written by Kathleen Knutson Howell (with rewrites by Coppola and Hinton). How *The Outsiders* got made into a movie is an interesting story. In March 1980, several months before anyone approached Hinton with the idea to make *Tex* into a movie, some kids from the Lone Star School in Fresno, California, wrote a letter to the famous director Francis Ford Coppola, asking him to consider making *The Outsiders* into a movie.

Fortunately for them, the kids sent the letter to the wrong address. They sent it to Paramount Pictures, which was the right studio, but instead of sending it to the production offices in Hollywood, they sent the letter to the corporate headquarters in New York City. The corporate headquarters was where all of the business affairs of the studio went on, not where people actually made movies. Coppola happened to be in New York at the time, and since he didn't get much mail there, he decided to read the letter himself. If the letter had gone to Hollywood, it would have ended up in a big pile of unread mail that probably would not have gotten to him.

Coppola's reaction, producer Fred Roos said in an article, was something along the lines of "Look at that cute letter. I bet kids have a good idea of what should be a movie. Check it out, if you want to."[5] Well, Roos decided to give *The Outsiders* a chance. He wasn't excited at first—he thought the book jacket was tacky, "like the book had been privately printed by some religious organization"[6]—so he thought he would read ten pages and see if the book was any good. He ended up reading it cover to cover in one sitting, and just like the students of Lone Star School, Roos thought it would make a good movie, too.

In the summer of 1980, Roos went to Oklahoma to talk to Hinton, and she agreed to sell Coppola the rights to make the movie. (A week later, Disney approached her about the rights to *Tex*.) According to Hinton, she had "never planned to sell the movie rights to my books. They mean so much to a lot of kids that I didn't want to see them messed up."[7] But she had seen *The Black Stallion*, adapted from Walter Farley's book by Coppola's studio, and she was pleased with the job they had done.

Still, she wasn't sure about Coppola until they began working together. Once Coppola visited her in Tulsa—to show her how he was writing the screenplay—she was totally convinced he could make the movie. He showed her how he had broken down the book into passages of action and passages of introspection or thought, and how he was using that breakdown to write the screenplay.

Hinton was impressed. Coppola, for his part, said in an article, "When I met Susie, it was confirmed to me that she was not just a young people's novelist, but a real American novelist. For me a primary thing about her books is that the characters come across as very real. Her dialogue is memorable, and her prose is striking. Often a paragraph of descriptive prose sums up something essential and stays with you."[8] Thus began a working relationship between Coppola and Hinton that would last for two movies.

Hinton got very involved with the making of *The Outsiders*, and she was an important presence on the set. Among other things, Coppola depended on her as "a security blanket and expert on things 'Southwestern,'"[9] as one Zoetrope (Coppola's production company) executive put it. She was paid as a consultant for her help. Not only that, but she continued her acting career with another cameo role. In *The Outsiders*, Hinton plays a nurse.

Before the movie came out, the students from Lone Star School, who were now high school juniors and seniors, were treated to a preview screening. The film's stars came and met the kids who had helped to make the film possible in the first place. And Jo Ellen Misakian, the librarian who organized the letter-writing campaign, received a standing ovation.

This movie was not as faithful to the book as *Tex* was. Part of the reason was Coppola's vision for the movie. As Jay Daly wrote in the book *Presenting S. E. Hinton*, "Coppola tried to expand the movie into something like myth, into a statement about youth and America, and unfortunately the continuity of the story got lost somewhere (probably on the cutting room floor)."[10]

Even though, in the attempt to make the story more universal, it got muddled, the movie has it fans—especially among people who have already read the book and know the story pretty well.

8 More Movies

The movie *Rumble Fish* grew out of the making of *The Outsiders*. Halfway through the filming of *The Outsiders*, Coppola, pleased with how things were going, asked Hinton if she had another novel he could make into a movie. She told him about *Rumble Fish* and Coppola got excited about the idea. He proposed that they write the screenplay on their days off, Sundays, then take a two week break after *The Outsiders* was finished before starting work on *Rumble Fish*.

Hinton said that Coppola's working style took some getting used to. (He liked to work

67

almost nonstop and assumed that everyone else could, too.) This was her reaction: "I said 'Sure, Francis, we're working 16 hours a day and you want to spend Sundays writing another screenplay?' But that's what we did."[1]

Hinton focused on the dialogue and Coppola focused on the visual images and structure. Hinton played a major role in the moviemaking process. As Coppola said, "Susie was a permanent member of the company. My experience with her made me realize that the notion of having a writer on the set makes a lot of sense."[2]

The result of all of that hard work, *Rumble Fish*, was released the same year as *The Outsiders* and starred Matt Dillon as Rusty-James. The film was shot in black and white to highlight Rusty-James's colorblindness. The only time color is used is when the fish of the title appear on screen. They are tinted in red and blue and they swim around onscreen in an effect that is both strange and wonderful. All in all, Coppola's risks paid off, and *Rumble Fish* the movie captures the mood and substance of *Rumble Fish* the novel.

Hinton's brief acting career came to a close with *Rumble Fish*. During a carnival-like city scene in the movie, Hinton has another cameo—she plays a streetwalker. That's not her voice, though—another actor's voice was added over hers in the studio.

Of the four films made from Hinton's novels, *That Was Then, This is Now* was the only one she was not involved with. (She also does not appear in the movie.) Emilio Estevez, an actor who had appeared in both *Tex* and *The Outsiders*, introduced his father, actor and producer Martin Sheen, to Hinton's novels. Sheen bought the rights to make the film, and Estevez went to work on the screenplay. The film, which stars Estevez as Mark Jennings, was released in 1985. Of all the films made from S. E. Hinton novels, this one is the least faithful to the book in terms of story line. The book is set in the wild, confusing late 1960s, but the movie does not concern itself with a specific period, instead aiming for a timeless feeling. Also, the book's hard-hitting ending is softened for the screen version.

Summing up her moviemaking experiences, Hinton had this to say: "It's the first time I've ever felt at home in a group situation. I've never been a joiner. In Tulsa, I have a reputation for being slightly eccentric. Even my close friends think I'm a little nutty. But with the movie people I was accepted instantly. I really like the way people support each other on a movie set. One of the guys on the crew who had been in Vietnam told me that making a movie is the closest thing to being in a battle that you can find in civilian life. You get the same camaraderie. Also, when you're making a movie, you feel like an outlaw. Traffic stops for you, and you don't keep the same hours that anybody else keeps. I like that outlaw feeling. And there's one other nice thing about movies. There's always somebody else to blame. With a novel, you have to take all the blame yourself."[3]

Hinton's movie adventures came to an end after *Rumble Fish* was made. Despite all of the glamour of moviemaking, including the pleasures of working with a star like Matt Dillon and a director like Francis Ford Coppola, and even the extra money earned from selling books to the silver screen, one gets the feeling that Hinton's "Hollywood Adventure" did not really change her much. She simply returned to normal life in Tulsa, and to her typewriter.

9 Children's Books and More

After *Taming the Star Runner*, Hinton focused again on family life and thought about the subject for a new novel. No story was calling out to her to be written, though this was not like the writer's block she experienced after *The Outsiders*. She was writing plenty; screenplays, television scripts, and advertisements were keeping her busy. Even after all of her Hollywood adventures, she was not interested in writing another novel. As Hinton explained, "I simply didn't have a story I wanted to tell."[1]

As a result, her next projects were a bit of a departure. She wrote two books for younger readers, *Big David, Little David* and *The Puppy Sister*, both published in 1995. The ideas for both of these books came from experiences she had with her son Nick when he was a little boy.

The idea for *Big David, Little David* came from a joke Hinton and her husband played on Nick on his first day of school. The book uses their real names. Nick meets a boy on his first day of school whose name is David, the same name as Nick's father. This boy also has dark hair and glasses, just like Nick's father. So Nick asks his father if the boy at school and he (his father) are the same person. And—this is where the joke comes in— his father tells him that the boy at school *is* him, that he and the boy are the same person. (See the interview with Hinton at the back of this book for more on this practical joke.) The book is a funny take on Nick trying to figure out who is who.

The Puppy Sister was a result of the family's experience with a new puppy. Hinton has called it the most autobiographical of all her novels. She said, "Nick is an only child and was not an animal person. He was a bit afraid of dogs, but I was determined to get him a puppy so he could connect and share attention in the family. We got our puppy when Nick was eight, and there was so much sibling rivalry between the two that he once accused me of loving the dog more than I loved him."[2] In observing Nick's competition with the puppy, Hinton saw a good idea for a book about a boy and his puppy. Nick provided the twist that made the book fun. He came home one day and asked Hinton when the puppy was going to turn into a real person.

These two books reflect a shift in focus for Hinton—from the turbulent world of teenage rebels, misfits, and gang members to the more domestic world of raising a child. Does this mean Hinton will never return to writing young adult novels? Who knows? In any case, it is kind of ironic that Hinton's novels, which have been almost universally praised for their gritty realism, are made-up stories, and that her two children's books, both of them somewhat weird and fantastic, are based on real-life events.

It is not surprising that Hinton's work has shifted to reflect changes in her life. She has never been the kind of writer who follows trends, or who tries to figure out what the next hot thing will be. She writes what she wants to write, and that strategy has worked out very well for her.

In our complex world, where it is easy to get distracted by every new thing, where it might seem smart to jump on every new trend, Hinton has remained true to those things that have always mattered to her. This, in itself, is an achievement, and her books, with their millions of loyal readers, are a testament to that achievement.

Interview with S. E. Hinton

This interview with S. E. Hinton was conducted by Tom Bodett for the nationally syndicated public radio series, "The Loose Leaf Book Company," produced by Ben Manilla Productions, Inc., of San Francisco. For more of this interview, visit www.looseleaf.org.

TOM BODETT: When you walk into a bookstore and see the sign over a section of books labeled young adults, it's important to understand that you wouldn't have seen a sign like that thirty years ago. The genre didn't even exist, at least in any form we'd recognize today, until an author named S. E. Hinton published the now classic novel *The Outsiders*. The gritty story of gang violence and adolescent alienation set the gold standard for young adult fiction.

Hinton, just sixteen years old when *The Outsiders* was written, went on to write four more young adult novels, which earned the author a wall full of national awards and several film adaptations, two from the renowned director, Francis Ford Coppola.

Before we speak with S. E. Hinton about *The Outsiders*, here's a passage from the book. It happens to be the very last paragraph of the story. "I sat down and picked up my pen and thought for a minute, remembering. Remembering a handsome dark boy with a reckless grin and a hot temper, a tough tow-headed boy with a cigarette in his mouth and a bitter grin on his hard face. Remembering, and this time it didn't hurt. A quiet, defeated-looking sixteen-year-old, whose hair needed cutting badly, and who had black eyes with a frightened expression to them. One week had taken all three of them and I decided I could tell people, beginning with my English teacher. I wondered for a long time how to start that theme, how to start writing about something that was important to me. And, I finally began like this: When I stepped down into the bright from the darkness of the movie house, I had only two things on my mind, Paul Newman and a ride home."

Well, Ms. Hinton, welcome to the Loose Leaf Book Company.

S. E. HINTON: Thanks.

TOM BODETT: These last two lines are of course the first two lines of your story as well. So when you were sixteen and you wrote those final circular words, did you have any notion of the forces that you just set in motion in your own life?

S. E. HINTON: Well, no, actually I didn't have any idea of getting it published. It was just another thing that I was writing.

TOM BODETT: And your second book, *That Was Then, This Is Now*, was that one difficult to write after doing something as successful as *The Outsiders* to follow up with that?

S. E. HINTON: Oh yes. I was in a complete state of writer's block for four years before I wrote again after *The Outsiders*. And let me say this, I think *That Was Then* is a better written book. It doesn't hit the emotional intensity that *The Outsiders* does. Even four years later, it was too late for me to be the same writer that wrote *The Outsiders*.

But, *That Was Then* was hard. I did it two pages a day and the only reason I did it was my boyfriend was sick of me being depressed and said start writing. "Who cares if you get published, two pages a day couldn't kill you, just do them." He would come over to take me out and if I hadn't done them, I didn't get to go out. So, that is my great motivation for writing *That Was Then, This Is Now*.

TOM BODETT: You needed a taskmaster there.

S. E. HINTON: Yes, and I ended up marrying the guy.

TOM BODETT: And so he's still the taskmaster.

S. E. HINTON: That's right. He's a mathematician and I can't add. He doesn't read. We get along great. He's the only one I let read things as I'm writing because I can always count on him to say "that's nice, honey," and that's all I want to hear.

TOM BODETT: Ms. Hinton, you are lauded for the clarity of the voice that you strike in your stories. Now it is thirty years later and you're writing picture books for younger children.

Why that change? Is there some new voice you've had to discover to do this?

S. E. HINTON: Well, I always begin with my narrator. I just really have to be that person. When I wrote my picture book, it's actually a true story based on a trick my husband was playing on our poor child when he started kindergarten. And my editor is the one that suggested I write it up for a picture book.

TOM BODETT: Well, what was this practical joke?

S. E. HINTON: When my little boy came home from his first day of kindergarten he looked at his dad and said, "Dad, there's a kid in my class and his name is David like you and he has dark hair like you and he wears glasses like you. Is that you?" My husband, you know, said, "Sure, Nick, that's me. Every day I get little and go to school with you." It freaked Nick out.

And, David really got into this and I have to admit I aided and abetted him by picking Nick up from kindergarten and saying "What happened, honey?" and [he'd say that] Kelsey threw up. I'd go home and sit him in front of the TV and run to the phone and say "David, Kelsey threw up." David would come home and say, "Well, Nick, weren't you grossed out when Kelsey threw up?" And Nick would just freak.

TOM BODETT: How long did you keep this up?

S. E. HINTON: Almost a year. It ruined any chance of the poor kid having a friendship with little David. But, we figured, heck, we'd given the kid something to tell the therapist when he's forty.

TOM BODETT: So besides giving you that story, just in general, did having children of your own affect your writing in a tangible way?

S. E. HINTON: It certainly did because I used to be able to say "Look, I'm not a parent, a teacher, or a cop. I'm on their side." Well, sorry, now I'm a parent. So, even when I'm writing a bad parent now, I'm secretly thinking "Oh, poor things, they're probably doing the best they can."

TOM BODETT: Our guest is S. E. Hinton, the author of *The Outsiders*, *That Was Then, This Is*

Now, several other titles for young adults. And now, *Big David, Little David* and *The Puppy Sister* for younger readers. And Ms. Hinton, looking way back, how tired are you of talking about *The Outsiders*?

S. E. HINTON: Well, after thirty years, after writing the book four times, after working on the screenplay, after working on the play version, after working on the TV series, I could throw up.

TOM BODETT: So my follow-up question is what do you think of your books now? I guess you've answered.

S. E. HINTON: No, *The Outsiders* I'm very proud of. It's almost like it was meant to be. I can't tell you how many letters I have from people saying it changed their life. It's been translated into twenty languages. It really has meant something to so many people. No, I don't have any contempt for it. I personally could not do that kind of good that that book has done, especially for getting people to read that don't like to read. It absolutely floors me. I get that day in and day out: "I didn't like to read, but then I read this book." It's more that

I'm bored with me personally having written *The Outsiders* than I'm bored with *The Outsiders*. It still amazes me the kind of effect it seems to have on people.

Timeline

1950 S. E. Hinton is born on July 22, in Tulsa, Oklahoma.

1967 *The Outsiders* is published.

1968 Hinton's short story "Rumble Fish" is published in *Nimrod* magazine, the literary supplement to the *University of Tulsa Alumni Magazine*.

1970 Hinton receives a bachelor of science degree from the University of Tulsa, majoring in education; she marries David E. Inhofe.

1971 *That Was Then, This Is Now* is published.

1975 *Rumble Fish*, the novel, is published.

1979 *Tex* is published.

1980 Hinton sells the film rights for *The*

Outsiders (to Zoetrope Studios) and *Tex* (to Disney Studios).

1982 *Tex*, the movie, is released in September.

1983 Hinton's son, Nicholas David Inhofe, is born in August. The movie version of *The Outsiders* is released in March, followed by *Rumble Fish*, which is released in October.

1985 *That Was Then, This Is Now*, the movie, is released in November.

1988 *Taming the Star Runner* is published; Hinton receives the first-ever YASD/SLJ Margaret A. Edwards Award, given by the Young Adult Services Division of the American Library Association and *School Library Journal*.

1995 Hinton's *Big David, Little David* and *The Puppy Sister*, two children's books, are published.

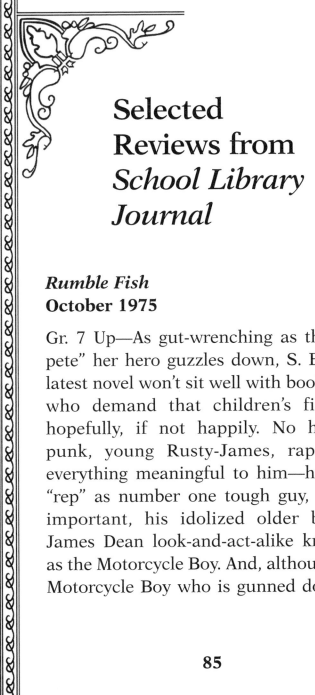

Selected Reviews from *School Library Journal*

Rumble Fish
October 1975

Gr. 7 Up—As gut-wrenching as the "sneaky pete" her hero guzzles down, S. E. Hinton's latest novel won't sit well with book selectors who demand that children's fiction end hopefully, if not happily. No hard-nosed punk, young Rusty-James, rapidly loses everything meaningful to him—his girl, his "rep" as number one tough guy, and, most important, his idolized older brother—a James Dean look-and-act-alike known only as the Motorcycle Boy. And, although it is the Motorcycle Boy who is gunned down at the end after breaking into a pet store, it is Rusty-James, emotionally burnt out at fourteen, who is the ultimate victim. Stylistically superb (the purposefully flat, colorless narrative exactly describes Rusty-James' turf of pool halls, porno movie houses, and seedy hangouts), this packs a punch that will leave readers of any age reeling. —Jane Abramson

Tex
November 1979

Gr. 6–10—Hinton's style has matured since she exploded on to the YA scene in 1967 with *The Outsiders* (Viking). In *Tex*, the raw energy for which Hinton has justifiably reaped praise has not been tamed—its been cultivated, and the result is a fine, solidly constructed and well-paced story. Fourteen-year-old Tex lives with his seventeen-year-old brother, Mason, in a rural area. Their father hasn't been home in five months and the relationship between the boys is tense. Each has his own problems, fears, and growing pains which keep him alienated, until a dramatic and terrifying experience forces them to seek comfort and support from each other. With Tex, Mason, their father, friends, and neighbors, Hinton has created a cast of distinct personalities. Personal discoveries emerge from the action in a natural, unpretentious, and nondidactic way as Hinton explores questions about responsibility, friendship, desire, and communication. —Marilyn Kaye, University of Chicago, Chicago, Illinois

Taming the Star Runner
October 1988

Gr 7–10—Devoted fans will leap on Hinton's new novel, yet her protagonist Travis is no *Tex* (Delacorte, 1979). On the surface, this fifteen-year-old resembles the classic misfits from the author's previous books; however, Travis lacks Tex's zest for living. Released from juvenile hall to cool down at his uncle's Oklahoma horse ranch, he acts the role of sensitive punk, he looks like a rebel and flies into violent rages, yet he seeks to publish his novel and he loves his cat. He wants to be left alone, but he suffers from being ignored by the "hicks" at school. The high point of his introspective retreat is his attraction to Casey, the riding instructor who leases his uncle's barn. The scenes of stable chores, riding lessons, and horse shows may interest some readers, while the equestrian jargon will mean nothing to the book's primary audience. Hinton uses a horse, Star Runner, as a counterpart to Travis to illustrate her theme of life's quirks: some win, some don't. Without making much of an effort, Travis ends up a winner—alive, free from jail, and a published author. Hinton builds a sparse plot around a predominately bleak theme. Although the story isn't fleshed out, tough-guy Travis will appeal to a certain readership. Others will find him forgettable, especially compared to his fictional predecessors. —Charlene Strickland, formerly at Albuquerque Public Library, New Mexico

List of Works

The Outsiders. New York: Viking Press, 1967.
That Was Then, This Is Now. New York: Viking Press, 1971.
Rumble Fish. New York: Delacorte Press, 1975.
Tex. New York: Delacorte Press, 1979.
Taming the Star Runner. New York: Delacorte Press, 1988.
Big David, Little David, illustrated by Alan Daniel. New York: Doubleday, 1995.
The Puppy Sister, illustrated by Jacqueline Rogers. New York: Delacorte Press, 1995.

List of Awards

ALA YASD/SLJ Margaret A. Edwards Award,
   given by the Young Adult Services Division
   of the American Library Association and
   School Library Journal (1988)
Golden Archer Award (1983)

The Outsiders (1967)
American Library Association Best Books for
   Young Adults citation (1975)
Chicago Tribune Book World Spring Book
   Festival Honor Book (1967)
Massachusetts Children's Book Award (1979)
Media and Methods Maxi Award (1975)
New York Herald Tribune's Best Teenage Books
   citation (1967)

That Was Then, This Is Now (1971)
American Library Association Best Books for
   Young Adults citation (1971)

Chicago Tribune Book World Spring Book Festival
Award Honor Book (1971)
Massachusetts Children's Book Award (1978)

Rumble Fish (1975)
American Library Association Best Books for
Young Adults citation (1975)
School Library Journal Best Books of the Year
citation (1975)
New Mexico Library Association Land of
Enchantment Book Award (1982)

Tex (1979)
American Book Award nomination for children's
paperback (1981)
American Library Association Best Books for
Young Adults citation (1979)
California Reading Association's California Young
Reader Medal nomination (1982)
Louisiana Association of School Libraries Sue
Hefly Award Honor Book (1982)
New York Public Library Books for the
Teen-Age citation (1980)
School Library Journal Best Books of the Year
citation (1979)

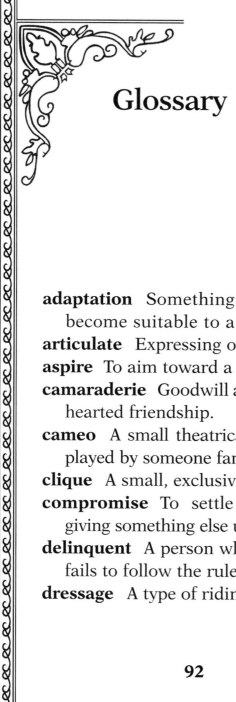

Glossary

adaptation Something that is changed to become suitable to a special use.

articulate Expressing oneself clearly.

aspire To aim toward a specific goal.

camaraderie Goodwill among friends; light-hearted friendship.

cameo A small theatrical or cinematic role, played by someone famous.

clique A small, exclusive group of friends.

compromise To settle for something by giving something else up.

delinquent A person who breaks the law or fails to follow the rules.

dressage A type of riding in which the rider

guides his or her horse through a series of maneuvers.

empathy The ability to share another's thoughts, emotions, or feelings.

fluke An accidental stroke of good luck.

foray An initial attempt at something.

genre A specific category (of literature).

hone To improve.

ironic Opposite to what is or might be expected.

malice An active desire to hurt others.

motivation Something that drives someone to action.

narrator The character who tells a story.

phenomenon An unusual or remarkable fact or occurrence.

prevail To be widespread or common.

prose Ordinary writing, without poetic structure.

reformatory A prison for youths and first-time offenders.

rival A competitor.

royalties The share of the money made from a book's sales that are paid to the author.

sensationalist Using shock, horror, or exaggeration to get a reaction.

sentimental Playing on one's emotions to get a response.

sibling rivalry Competition between brothers and/or sisters.

tangent A sudden change of direction.

writer's block A usually temporary condition in which a writer finds himself or herself unable to write.

wry Dry humor, often with a touch of irony.

For More Information

Web Sites

Due to the changing nature of Internet links, the Rosen Publishing Group, Inc., has developed an online list of Web sites related to the subject of this book. This site is updated regularly. Please use this link to access the list:

http://www.rosenlinks.com/lab/sehi/

For Further Reading

Daly, Jay. *Presenting S. E. Hinton*. Boston: Twayne Publishers, 1989.
This excellent book remains the best source for more information about S. E. Hinton, and includes a great deal of insight into the themes and characters of Hinton's novels.

Bibliography

Andrews, Sheryl. Review of *That Was Then, This Is Now*. *Horn Book*, July–August 1971, p. 338.

Campbell , Patty. Review of *Taming the Star Runner*. *New York Times Book Review*, April 2, 1989, p. 26.

Campbell, Patty. "The Young Adult Perplex." *Wilson Library Bulletin*, September 1985, p. 62.

Cart, Michael. Review of *That Was Then, This Is Now*. *New York Times Book Review*, August 8, 1971, p. 8.

Daly, Jay. *Presenting S.E. Hinton*. Boston: Twayne Publishers, 1989.

de Montreville, Doris and Elizabeth J. Crawford, eds. *Fourth Book of Junior*

Authors. H.W. Wilson, 1978. Reprinted at http://www.edupaperback.org/ authorbios/Hinton_SE.html. Retreived April 2002.

Ehrichs, Lisa. "Advice from a Penwoman." *Seventeen*, Vol. 40, November 1981, p. 32.

"Face to Face with a Teen-Age Novelist," *Seventeen*, October 1967.

Farber, Stephen. "Directors Join the S.E. Hinton Fan Club." *New York Times*, March 20, 1983, Sec. 2, p. 19.

Fisher, Margery. Review of *Tex. Growing Point*, May 1980, pp. 3686–3687.

Fisher, Margery. Review of *Rumble Fish. Growing Point*, May 1976, p. 2894.

Fleming, Thomas. Review of *The Outsiders. New York Times Book Review*, May 1967, Part 2, pp. 10–12.

Harmetz, Aljean. "Making *The Outsiders*, A Librarian's Dream." *New York Times*, March 23, 1983.

Hentoff, Nat. Review of *The Outsiders. Atlantic Monthly*, December 1967.

Hinton, Hal. "Writer of 'Tex' is comfortable dealing with Disney and Coppola." *Chicago Tribune*, December 24, 1982, Sec. 3, p. 7.

Hinton, Susan. "Teen-Agers Are for Real." *New York Times Book Review*, August 27, 1967, p. 26.

Hinton, S. E., and Donald R. Gallo, ed. *Speaking For Ourselves*. Urbana, IL: National Council of Teachers of English, 1990, p. 96.

Hinton, S. E. The Official S. E. Hinton Website. Retrieved April 2002 (http://www.sehinton.com).

Hinton, S. E. "S. E. Hinton: On Writing Tex." *Delacorte Press Notes*, Delacorte Press. Reprinted on the Internet School Library Media Center S. E. Hinton page. Retrieved March 2002 (http://falcon.jmu.edu/~ramseyil/hinton.htm).

Hinton, S. E. *Big David, Little David*, illustrated by Alan Daniel. New York: Doubleday, 1995.

Hinton, S. E. *The Outsiders*. New York: Viking Press, 1967.

Hinton, S. E. *The Puppy Sister*, illustrated by Jacqueline Rogers. New York: Delacorte, 1995.

Hinton, S. E. *Rumble Fish*. New York: Delacorte Press, 1975.

Hinton, S. E. *Taming the Star Runner*. New York: Delacorte Press, 1988.

Hinton, S. E. *Tex.* New York: Delacorte Press, 1979.

Hinton, S. E. *That Was Then, This is Now.* New York: Viking Press, 1971.

Kaye, Marilyn. Review of *Tex.* *School Library Journal*, November 1979, p. 88.

Kirkus Reviews, October 15, 1975, p. 1193.

Litchfield, Yvonne. "Her Book to Be Published Soon, But Tulsa Teen-Ager Keeps Cool." *Tulsa Daily World*, April 7, 1967, p. 20.

Loer, Stephanie. "Bringing Realism to Teen-Age Fiction." *Boston Globe*, August 31, 1988, p. 69.

Plemons, Linda. "Author Laureate of Adolescent Fiction." *University of Tulsa Annual*, 1983–1984.

Powell, Jane. "Urban Guerrillas." *Times Literary Supplement*, April 2, 1976, p. 388.

Publisher's Weekly. July 28, 1975, p. 122.

Smith, Dave. "Hinton: What Boys Are Made Of." *Los Angeles Times*, July 15, 1982, p. 27.

Strickland, Charlene. Review of *Taming the Star Runner. School Library Journal*, Vol. 35, No. 2, October 1988, p. 161.

"Susie Loves Matt." *American Film*, April
    1983, p. 34.

Sutherland, Zena. "The Teen-Ager Speaks." *The
    Saturday Review*, January 27, 1968, p. 34.

Teachers@Random, "S. E. Hinton." Retrieved
    May 2002. (http://www.randomhouse.com/
    teachers/authors/sehi.html).

Source Notes

Introduction
1. Doris de Montreville and Elizabeth J. Crawford, editors, *Fourth Book of Junior Authors*. (H.W. Wilson, 1978).
2. "Susie Loves Matt," *American Film*, April 1983, p. 34.

Chapter 1
1. Doris de Montreville and Elizabeth J. Crawford, editors, *Fourth Book of Junior Authors*. (H.W. Wilson, 1978).
2. Ibid.
3. Lisa Ehrichs, "Advice from a Penwoman," *Seventeen*, Vol. 40, November 1981, p. 32.

4. Ibid, p. 32.

5. Yvonne Litchfield, "Her Book to Be Published Soon, But Tulsa Teen-Ager Keeps Cool," *Tulsa Daily World*, April 7, 1967, p. 20.

Chapter 2

1. "Face to Face with a Teen-Age Novelist," *Seventeen*, October 1967.

2. S. E. Hinton, "S. E. Hinton: On Writing Tex," *Delacorte Press Notes*, Delacorte Press.

3. Robert Frost, "Nothing Gold Can Stay," reprinted in S. E. Hinton, *The Outsiders* (New York: Puffin Books [Penguin], 1997), p. 77.

4. Patty Campbell, "The Young Adult Perplex," *Wilson Library Bulletin*, September 1985, p. 62.

5. Nat Hentoff, review of *The Outsiders*, *Atlantic Monthly*, December, 1967.

6. Thomas Fleming, review of *The Outsiders*, *New York Times Book Review*, May 1967, Part 2, pp. 10–12.

7. Zena Sutherland, "The Teen-Ager Speaks," *The Saturday Review*, January 27, 1968, p. 34.

8. Susan Hinton, "Teen-Agers Are for Real," *New York Times Book Review*, August 27, 1967, p. 26.

9. Lisa Ehrichs, "Advice from a Penwoman," *Seventeen*, Vol. 40, November 1981, p. 32.

Chapter 3

1. Patty Campbell, "The Young Adult Perplex," *Wilson Library Bulletin*, September 1985, p. 62.
2. Linda Plemons, "Author Laureate of Adolescent Fiction," *University of Tulsa Annual*, 1983–1984.
3. Doris de Montreville and Elizabeth J. Crawford, editors, *Fourth Book of Junior Authors*. (H.W. Wilson, 1978).
4. Quoted in Jay Daly, *Presenting S. E. Hinton* (Boston: Twayne Publishers, 1989).
5. Michael Cart, review of *That Was Then, This Is Now*, *New York Times Book Review*, August 8, 1971, p. 8.
6. Sheryl Andrews, review of *That Was Then, This Is Now*, *Horn Book*, July/August 1971, p. 338.

Chapter 4

1. Linda Plemons, "Author Laureate of Adolescent Fiction," *University of Tulsa Annual*, 1983–1984.
2. Q&A from http://www.sehinton.com.
3. Teachers@Random, http://www.randomhouse.com/teachers/authors/sehi.html.
4. Dave Smith, "Hinton: What Boys Are Made Of," *Los Angeles Times*, July 15, 1982, p. 27.
5. *Publisher's Weekly*, July 28, 1975, p. 122.
6. *Kirkus Reviews*, October 15, 1975, p. 1193.
7. Jane Powell, "Urban Guerrillas," *Times Literary Supplement*, April 2, 1976, p. 388.

8. Margery Fisher, review of *Rumble Fish*, *Growing Point*, May 1976, p. 2894.

9. Jay Daly, *Presenting S. E. Hinton* (Boston: Twayne Publishers, 1989), pp. 67–68.

Chapter 5

1. S. E. Hinton, "S.E. Hinton: On Writing Tex," *Delacorte Press Notes*, Delacorte Press.

2. Ibid.

3. Linda Plemons, "Author Laureate of Adolescent Fiction," *University of Tulsa Annual*, 1983–1984.

4. Dave Smith, "Hinton: What Boys Are Made Of," *Los Angeles Times*, July 15, 1982, p. 27.

5. S. E. Hinton, *Tex* (New York: Delacorte Press, 1979), Laurel Leaf Library Edition, p. 35.

6. Marilyn Kaye, review of *Tex*, *School Library Journal*, November 1979, p. 88.

7. Margery Fisher, review of *Tex*, *Growing Point*, May 1980, pp. 3686–3687.

Chapter 6

1. Patty Campbell, "The Young Adult Perplex," *Wilson Library Bulletin*, September 1985, p. 61.

2. Teachers@Random, http://www.randomhouse.com/teachers/authors/sehi.html.

3. S. E. Hinton, in *Speaking For Ourselves*, Donald R. Gallo, ed. (Urbana, IL: National Council of Teachers of English, 1990), p. 96.

4. Charlene Strickland, review of *Taming the Star

Runner, School Library Journal, Vol. 35, No. 2, October 1988, p. 161.

5. Patty Campbell, review of *Taming the Star Runner*, *New York Times Book Review*, April 2, 1989, p. 26.

6. Ibid, p. 26.

7. Stephanie Loer, "Bringing Realism to Teen-Age Fiction," *Boston Globe*, August 31, 1988, p. 69.

Chapter 7

1. Hal Hinton, "Writer of 'Tex' is comfortable dealing with Disney and Coppola," *Chicago Tribune*, December 24, 1982, Sec. 3, p. 7.

2. Stephen Farber, "Directors Join the S. E. Hinton Fan Club," *New York Times*, March 20, 1983, Sec. 2, p. 19.

3. "Susie Loves Matt," *American Film*, April 1983, p. 34.

4. Ibid.

5. Aljean Harmetz, "Making 'The Outsiders,' A Librarian's Dream," *New York Times*, March 23, 1983.

6. Ibid.

7. Hinton, p. 7.

8. Farber article.

9. Hinton, p. 7.

10. Jay Daly, *Presenting S. E. Hinton* (Boston: Twayne Publishers, 1989), p. 133.

Chapter 8

1. Stephen Farber, "Directors Join the S. E. Hinton Fan Club," *New York Times*, March 20, 1983, Sec. 2, p. 19.
2. Ibid, p. 19.
3. Ibid, p. 19.

Chapter Nine

1. Teachers@Random, http://www.randomhouse.com/teachers/authors/sehi.html.
2. Ibid.

Index

About the Author

Antoine Wilson is the author of *The Young Zillionaire's Guide to Distributing Goods and Services*, *Family Matters: You and a Death in Your Family*, and *The Assassination of President McKinley*. He lives in southern California.

Photo Credits

Cover, p. 2 © Ed Lallo/Timepix.

Series Design and Layout

Tahara Hasan

Editor

Annie Sommers